The Ashford Book of

Weaving For Knitters

25 Easy Scarf Projects using Fancy Yarns and the Ashford Knitters Loom

Rowena Hart

Contents

Copyright © 2005, Ashford Handicrafts Limited.

All rights reserved. No part of this publication may be reproduced, stored in a retrieval system or transmitted in any form by any means electronic, mechanical, photocopying, recording or otherwise, without prior permission from the publisher.

ISBN: 0-958631-5-9

Printed in China by Book Builders through Willson Scott Publishing Limited, Christchurch, New Zealand
Email: publish@willsonscott.biz, www.willsonscott.biz

The Projects

14

Fun and Fancy

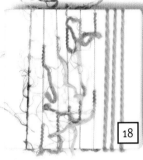

16

Party Party – 2 versions

18

Blue & Green

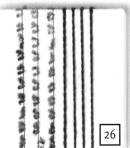

20

Two Neckpieces – 2 versions

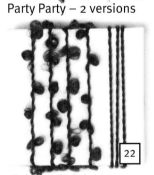

22

Violet and Violet

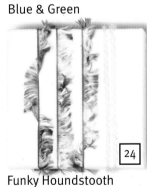

24

Funky Houndstooth

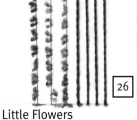

26

Little Flowers

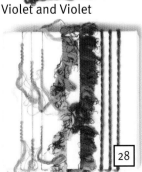

28

Seagrasses

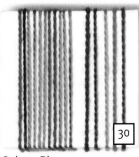

30

Colour Play

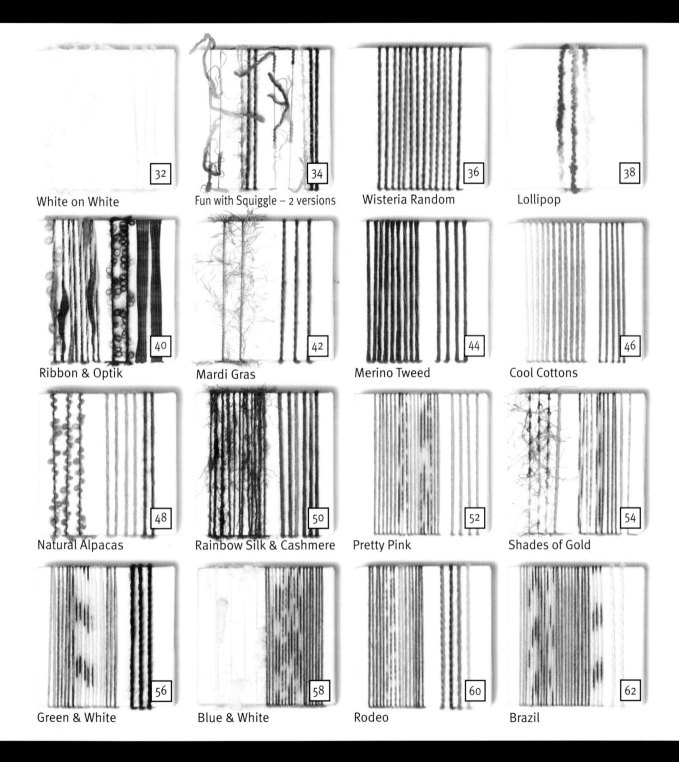

White on White 32

Fun with Squiggle – 2 versions 34

Wisteria Random 36

Lollipop 38

Ribbon & Optik 40

Mardi Gras 42

Merino Tweed 44

Cool Cottons 46

Natural Alpacas 48

Rainbow Silk & Cashmere 50

Pretty Pink 52

Shades of Gold 54

Green & White 56

Blue & White 58

Rodeo 60

Brazil 62

Foreword by Karen Selk

Karen is a master weaver and teacher, specialising in weaving silk. Karen Selk and Terry Nelson live on Salt Spring Island, Canada, where their business, Treenway Crafts, is based.

No matter how long one has been weaving, the memories of texture, smell, colours and feeling of pride in having made one's first piece of weaving remain strong and special. This is the thrilling journey on which you are about to embark.

Weaving is extremely practical and useful. There is an excitement in giving such things a personal flare through the artistic choice of yarns, texture, colour and how to put these together in the structure of the cloth.

The Rigid Heddle Loom is the easiest and fastest way to be introduced to the spell of weaving. The Ashford Knitters Loom is designed specifically to make your voyage into weaving easy, fast and convenient. Easy, because the loom is very simple to understand and operate. Fast, because Rowena's method of direct warping by-passes steps used in other warping procedures. The projects are technically simple and fast to weave, but have a sophisticated, fun bounce to them. Convenient, because we used yarn types readily available in most knitting or weaving stores.

We are pleased to welcome you to the exciting and satisfying world of weaving.

Calling All Knitters

All knitters love yarn. Weaving is an exciting way of playing with coloured and textured yarns in a very different way.

> It's easy
> It's fun
> It's quick

All you need is a loom, some simple tools and the yarn. In all these projects I used the Ashford Knitters Loom, a portable, folding loom ideal for weaving scarves.

Fold it up and take it with you, just like your knitting.

The Loom

It's easy to set-up the loom using my super-quick method. Using funky big yarns you can weave a beautiful scarf in an hour or so!

The complete "How to" guide is included in the loom kit.

All projects in this book were woven using a 7.5 dpi – 30/10 cm reed.

The Knitters Loom is available from craft and yarn stores around the world. For the name of your nearest store contact the distributor in your country. *(See inside back cover.)*

Warp & Weft

These are two terms you will come to know as they form the basis of all weaving.

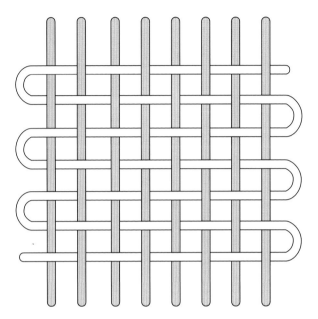

The **warp** threads are put onto the loom first. They are held on the loom under tension.

The **weft** rows pass over and under the warp threads to form the woven fabric.

In the projects I have used the term "the weaving" instead of "the weft".

The yarn used in the projects

I tried to use yarns that can be found in most yarn stores, or easily swapped for another brand.

Check the yardage and the fibre content. Don't be afraid to substitute.

Ask at your yarn store – they will be happy to help you.

Choosing the yarn

Wonderful fancy yarns

The new fancy yarns have wonderful names like Fiddle de dee, Moonlight, Tufty, Splash, Fizz, Whisper, DragonFly and my favourite – Squiggle!

Squiggle - A unique pigtail yarn

Most needed

As I worked my way through the projects, I realised that a smooth DK (double knit) Sportsweight yarn formed the framework for many of the projects. These yarns are offered everywhere in wool, alpaca, acrylic and many blends of wool/alpaca, wool/silk etc etc. The choice is endless.

I chose to use Tekapo DK Sportsweight yarn from Ashford as the plain yarn. It is 100% wool with a slightly textured handspun look, ideal for weaving, with a good colour range. The very bright colours were often needed to accent or enhance the projects.

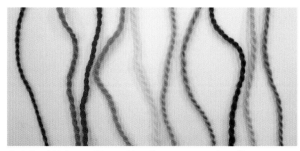

Ashford Tekapo Yarn. Use for warp and weft.

Eyelash yarns

There are several kinds of eyelash yarns. All are fabulous for accent and adding the "wow" factor to a work. Combine the finer eyelash with other yarns – they are not substantial enough to use on their own. The yarn with the long lashes sticks a bit in the warp but is good in the weft.

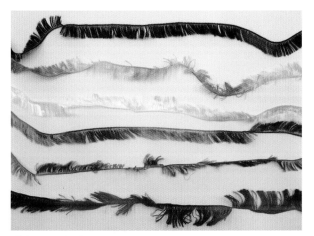

Shiny eyelash yarn

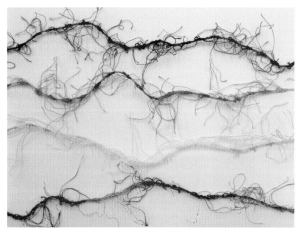

Finer eyelash yarn

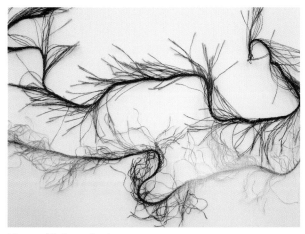

Yarn with long lashes

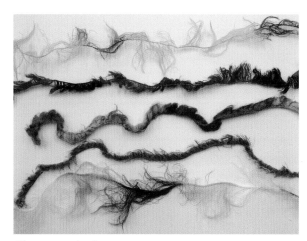

Shaggy eyelash yarn

Pigtail yarns

There are so many of these yarns available and more and more weird and wonderful new choices are reaching the stores every week. Use in the weft on their own or combined with a plain yarn.

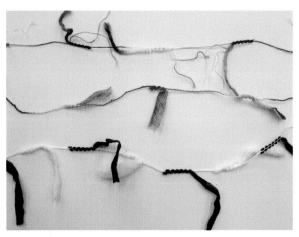

Pigtail yarns

Ribbon yarns

There are many kinds of ribbon yarns in silk, wool, acrylic and other fibres. Some are shiny, stripey, glittery and others are a ladder-like design. Use as accents in the warp and weft.

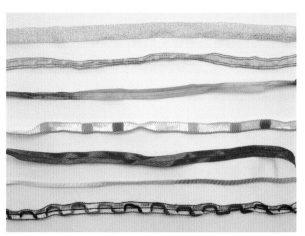

Ribbon yarn

Thick and thin

These yarns are suitable for using as weft, usually by themselves.

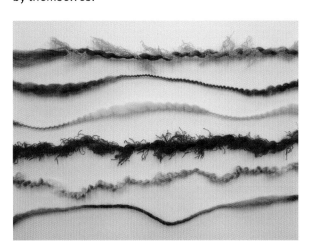

An idea

Ladder ribbon and a plain yarn combine well in a 2 x 2 pattern.

Brushed and boucle

Use the brushed yarns in the weft only. They tend to stick together if used in the warp.

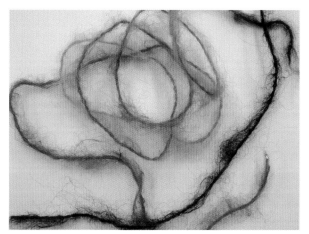

Brushed mohair and acrylic yarns

The finer boucles are suitable for warp and weft. The thicker boucle or loop yarns are best in the weft.

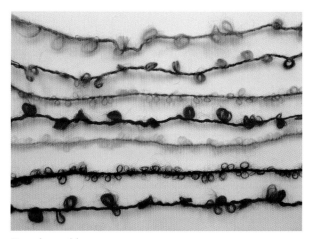

Boucle and loop yarns

Accent yarns

Use these yarns in combination with a plain yarn. Often these yarns have a percentage of metallic thread, which adds to the impact.

Two pretty accent yarns

Random colours

Make the most of the beautiful selection of hand-painted, hand-dyed, commercially-dyed, rainbow and random-colour yarns. Often, it is enough to use the same yarn for the whole project. Or try random-coloured yarns in the warp, take a shade from the random mix and weave it into the work and be amazed at the results you will achieve!

Beautiful hand-painted big loop yarn

A recycled silk yarn and a supersoft rayon/nylon mix in bright rainbow colours

Making your own Ball of Fancy Yarn

Most knitters and weavers have a variety of yarns on hand – leftovers, bargains, or yarn bought for a rainy day. So it's good to use some of these coveted yarns and make something different and original. Look in your stash!

Try this

Choose yarns that have shades of the same colour. Blue is an easy choice as many multi-coloured yarns have some blue content. Cut a length of each yarn – up to approx. 1 metre (1 yard). Short lengths are good – they will add interest to your scarf. Make a ball of yarn tying the lengths together – use an overhand knot to join (the same knot you use to knot a fringe). Some yarns are very fine: double them up or combine with another thread. This is a great thing to do with a group of friends. Get together with your box of yarns and soon you will be swapping yarns and the colours and textures will give you great ideas for future projects! You will need about 100 gms to weave one scarf.

When weaving with a stash ball of yarn you can choose to weave the ends at every knot where the yarn is joined either into the row or, take the knot and ends out onto the front of the weaving. I like to pull the ends out to make the colours and textures more visible.

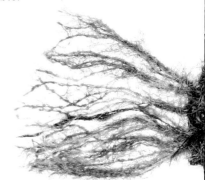

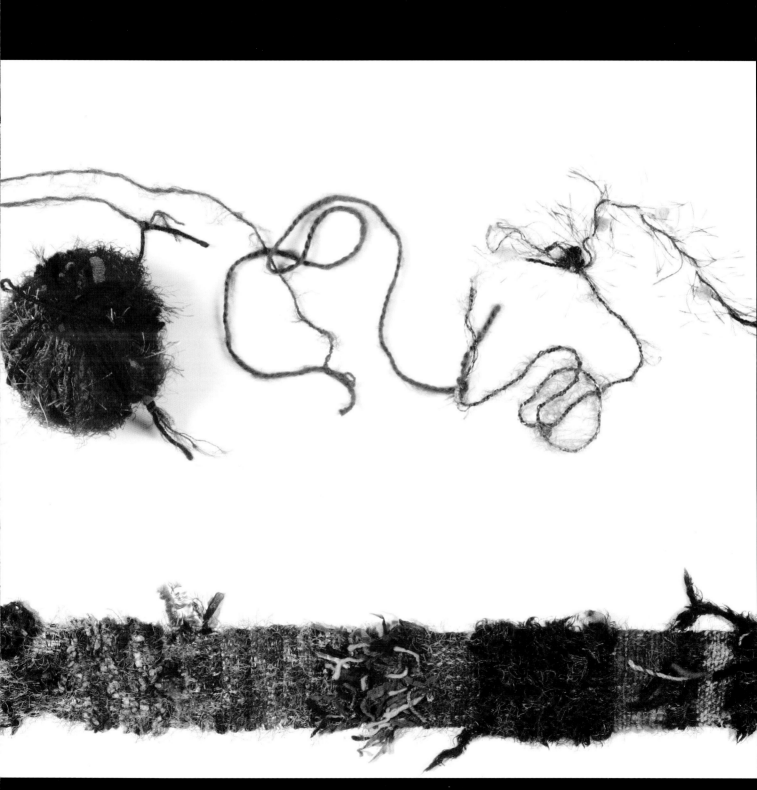

Beating

Always beat gently. Measure the rows per cm/inch recommended in each project. Sometimes the work will look a little open. Remember, the work is under tension on the loom and will come together when taken off. Also, the washing process will close the gaps a little.

Fixing a Broken Thread

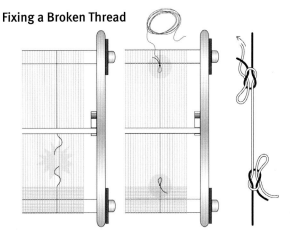

Sticky Warps

Some eyelash and mohair yarns stick together a little when used as a warp. Try this before giving up.

Down Weaving Position

Before weaving the row in the down position, take the reed to half way between the weaving and the support block – press down on the warp threads and across into the down position.

Up Weaving Position

Before weaving the row in the up position, tilt the reed forward, flat against the warp as you lift the reed into the upper position on the support block.

Do these two steps every row, you will get into a rhythm and it won't take any longer than usual.

Increase the warp tension

Warp Tension

The threads should be firm but not too tight. If the space for the shuttle does not open cleanly try increasing the warp tension.

Warping With Two Colours

Many of the projects use two colours in the warp. Tie both yarns to the back stick behind the slot you will thread first. Take the first colour through the reed and over the peg. Take the second colour through the reed and over the peg.

Continue in the usual way. This is much easier than cutting and tying the threads at each colour change.

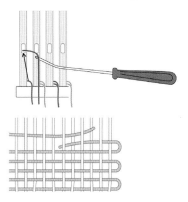

Joining a New Colour

Overlap the last and next thread.

Keeping the Colours Correct at the Edges

When meeting another colour at the edge always go around it.

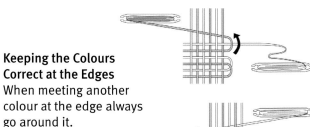

Finishing

Knotted Fringe

Lay your work on the table and tie the ends in groups of four. Use overhand knots.

Darn the end thread into your work using a wool needle.

Twisted Fringe

Separate out threads to be twisted i.e. four threads. Twist both sets of 2 threads to the right. It is a rolling action between the thumb and first two fingers.

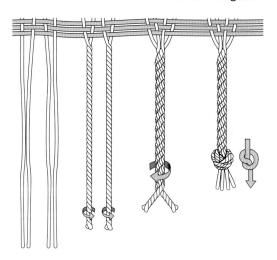

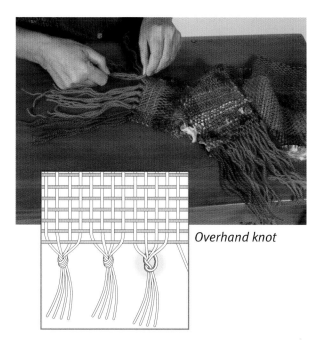

Overhand knot

Now twist both sets of two together in the opposite direction. Wind each set over and over until you have the look you want. Experiment. The more twist the lighter and narrower the cord will be. When you are happy with the look, tie an overhand knot at the end of the fringe to hold the twist in place. When finished all ends, you may wish to trim to neaten.

Washing

The woven work should be washed so the threads open up and fill the spaces to give the fabric a "finished" look.

Wash the scarf gently in warm water with a little detergent. Push up and down for $1/2$ a minute. Let the soapy water drain away and rinse the scarf in warm, clean water. Hang out to dry. Place the work over a towel so you don't get a fold line on the fabric. When the work is still damp, cover it with a soft cotton cloth and press with a warm iron. Hang again until thoroughly dry.

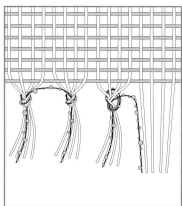

Adding fancy yarn to the fringe

Fast & Funky

Everyone loves a project that is quick and easy and looks fabulous. Don't be afraid to put bright colours together. Keep the weaving simple, using a smooth DK sportsweight warp and extra-bumpy yarns in the weaving to add to the funky look!

Fast & Funky | *1*   *Fun and Fancy*

This project is a great example of taking a funky yarn and just enjoying the different textures doing funky things as you weave. The bright pink in the background adds to the fun look!

Yarn Used:
Fizz from Crystal Palace – 110 m/120 yds = 50 gms
Parade from Classic Elite – 91.5 m/100 yds = 50 gms
Tekapo from Ashford – 200 m/218 yds = 100 gms

Quantity:
Fizz – 1 x 50 gm ball in Pink, colour # 9225
Parade – 1 x 50 gm ball in Green and Blue random, colour # 4547
Tekapo – approx. 30 gms in Teal, colour # 037

Warp:
Length – 190 cm (75 ins)
Number of ends – 38
Finished width – 12 cm (4 3/4 ins)

Warp Yarn:
Tekapo x 2 and Fizz x 2, repeat across warp, finish with Tekapo x 2. There will be Tekapo yarn at each edge.
(When making a warp with 2 colours, refer to page 12.)

The Weaving:
Use Parade throughout.
Beat softly – 3 rows to 2.5 cm (1 in.).

Finishing:
Tie ends in groups of 4 with a group of 5 at each edge.
Tie in overhand knots.

This is a very simple but bright and colourful project. Hot pink and red warps with very funky fancy fur make for an exciting result!

Yarn Used:
Tekapo from Ashford – 200 m/218 yds = 100 gms
Circus Fancy Fur from Wentworth – 35 m/39 yds = 50 gms

Quantity:
Version one
Tekapo – 50 gms in Bright Pink, colour # 021
Circus – 1 x 50 gm ball in Wild White, colour # 200

Version two
Tekapo – 50 gms in Traditional Red, colour # 008
Circus – 1 x 50 gm ball in Rainbow Red, colour # 213

Warp:
Length – 200 cm (79 ins)
Number of ends – 36
Finished width – 12 cm (4 ³/₄ ins)

Warp Yarn:
Use Tekapo throughout.

The Weaving:
Use Circus throughout.
Beat softly – 4 rows to 2.5 cm (1 in.).

Finishing:
Tie ends in groups of 4 with overhand knots.
Add some Circus into the fringe to colour it up and add to the party look. *(Refer to page 13.)*

Weaving a pigtail and smooth yarn together forms a background and shaggy surface at the same time.

Yarn Used:
Fizz from Crystal Palace – 110 m/120 yds = 50 gms
Squiggle from Crystal Palace – 91.5 m/100 yds = 50 gms
Tekapo from Ashford – 200 m/218 yds = 100 gms

Quantity:
Fizz – 50 gms in Key Lime, colour # 9224
Squiggle – 50 gms in Scuba Dive, colour # 9548
Tekapo – 75 gms in Lime, colour # 035

Warp:
Length – 190 cm (75 ins)
Number of ends – 38
Finished width – 12 cm (4 3/4 ins)

Warp Yarn:
Tekapo x 2 and Fizz x 2 repeat across warp, finish with Tekapo x 2. There will be Tekapo yarn at each edge.
(When making a warp with 2 colours, refer to page 12.)

The Weaving:
Wind Tekapo and Squiggle onto a shuttle together. Use these 2 yarns together throughout. Beat into a square weave. The rows in the weft measure the same as the warp rows across.
Lie one row into the work, PULL UP the shaggy, squiggle pigtail ends onto the front of the work before beating the row into place.
Beat 4 rows to 2.5 cm (1 in.).

Finishing:
Tie ends in groups of 4 with a group of 5 threads at each edge. Tie in overhand knots.

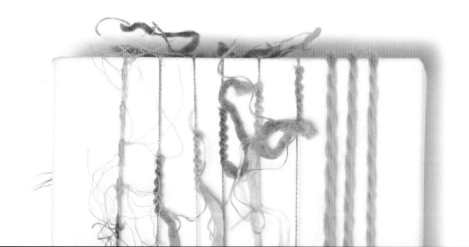

These two projects are super exotic-looking. They are a little shorter than a scarf, more of a neckpiece. Wear them low around your neck, secure with a pin. They look great with a little black dress!

Yarn Used:

Ostrich Fun Fur from Patons – 70 m/76 yds = 50 gms
Boucle from Lion – 52 m/57 yds = 70 gms
Temptation Fun Fur from Wentworth – 60 m/65 yds = 50 gms

Quantity:

Version one
Fun Fur – 1 x 50 gm ball in Bright Blue, colour # 106
Boucle – 1 x 70 gm ball in Sorbet, colour # 930-205

Version two
Fun Fur – 1 x 50 gm ball in Chocolate, colour # 126
Boucle – 1 x 70 gm ball in Tutti Fruitti, colour # 930-211

Warp:

Length – 140 cm (55 ins)
Number of ends – 36
Finished width – 13 cm (5 ins)

Warp Yarn:

Use Fun Fur throughout.

The Weaving:

Use Boucle throughout. Beat gently. 3 rows to 2.5 cm (1 in.). The Fun Fur may be a bit sticky in the warp. Keep a tight tension and beat in a different way.
(Refer to notes on beating – page 12.)
You may use your fingers now and then to open the space for the shuttle.
Take a little care – the result is worth the effort!

Finishing:

Tie ends in groups in 4 groups of 9 threads. Tie in overhand knots. Add some boucle to the fringe to give it a "party" look. *(Refer to page 13.)*

Stripes & Squares

Stripes and squares are seen in all aspects of design. We see them everywhere. The nature of weaving is to have a vertical and a horizontal thread so it naturally invites us to include stripes and squares in our woven pieces. In weaving we can use textures as well to form the design. Many traditional weaving patterns include squares as in project No. 2 which is a variation of a houndstooth check.

Stripes & Squares | 1 — *Violet and Violet*

The broad stripes of Violet yarns are worked in similar colours and both in mohair, but very different yarn types. One is a big loop yarn; the other is a smooth brushed yarn. A very easy and effective way to show off textures in weaving.

Yarn Used:
Loopy Mohair/Acrylic from Patons – 40 m/43 yds = 50 gms
Tekapo from Ashford – 200 m/218 yds = 100 gms
La Gran Mohair from Classic Elite – 83 m/90 yds = 42 gms

Quantity:
Loopy Mohair – 1 x 50 gm ball in Violet, colour # 11
Tekapo – 1/2 x 100 gm ball in Plum, colour # 010
La Gran Mohair – 1 x 50 gm ball in Plum, colour # 6579

Warp:
Length – 190 cm (75 ins)
Number of ends – 42
Finished width – 13.5 cm (5 1/4 ins)
The Loopy yarn stripes will be slightly wider than the brushed yarn.

Warp Yarn:
Use Tekapo throughout.

The Weaving:
Worked in wide stripes 19 cm (7 1/2 ins) each. Start with plain brushed yarn then the loopy. Alternate in 19 cm (7 1/2 ins) stripes to end. There will be 4 plain stripes and 3 loop yarn stripes.

Weaving Sequence

Plain	Loop	Plain	Loop	Plain	Loop	Plain

Start   Finish

Finishing:
Tie ends in groups of 7 using an overhand knot. Add Loopy yarn in to all knots across the fringe.
(Refer to page 13.)

This is a very traditional houndstooth check, where the warp and weft threads are alternated 2 and 2. Two smooth white threads beside two shiny blue eyelash threads are woven throughout. A new twist on a traditional pattern.

Yarn Used:
Boa from Bernat – 65 m/71 yds = 50 gms
Tekapo from Ashford – 200 m/218 yds = 100 gms

Quantity:
Boa – 1 x 50 gm ball in Blue, colour # 81106
Tekapo – 1 x 50 gm ball in Natural White

Warp:
Length – 190 cm (75 ins)
Number of ends – 38
Finished width – 12 cm (4 ¾ ins)

Warp Sequence:
Start with 2 White
　　　　　 2 Blue
Repeat until 36 ends are in place and add 2 more White, so the White will be at each edge.
(When making a warp with 2 colours, refer to page 12.)

The Weaving:
Wind one shuttle with the White and one with the Blue. Work 2 rows White and 2 rows Blue as follows:

Step 1　Using White yarn, start on the right hand side of the work, weave 2 rows.

Step 2　First Blue row. Start on the left hand side, weave 1 row – leave 3 cm (1 ¼ in.) of Blue out at beginning of row.

Step 3　Second Blue row. Take the Blue yarn around the White yarn at the edge and weave 1 row. Place Blue end into this same row.

Step 4　Weave 2 rows White.

Step 5　Weave 2 rows Blue

Repeat Steps 4 and 5 to end.
Note: Always go around the other colour when you meet it at each edge.
Start and finish the scarf with the White yarn.

Finishing:
Tie ends in groups of 4, 2 White and 2 Blue.
There will be 2 groups of 5, one at each edge.
Use overhand knots.

The combination of a smooth yarn and a pretty textured metallic yarn make a striking evening scarf. The pattern is the same as the previous scarf, Funky Houndstooth but looks very different.

Yarn Used:
Little Flowers from Crystal Palace – 132.5 m/145 yds = 50 gm
Tekapo from Ashford – 200 m/218 yds = 100 gms

Quantity:
Little Flowers – 1 x 50 gm ball in Flame, colour # 9551
Tekapo yarn – 1 x 50 gms of Plum, colour # 010

Warp:
Length – 190 cm (75 ins)
Number of ends – 26
Finished width – 10 cm (4 ins)

Warp Yarn:
Use Flame and Plum

Warp Sequence:
Start with 2 Plum
             2 Flame
Repeat until 24 ends are in place and add 2 more Plum, so the same colour is at each edge.
(When making a warp with 2 colours, refer to page 12.)

The Weaving:
Wind one shuttle with the Plum and one with the Flame colour. Work 2 rows Plum and 2 rows Flame throughout scarf. Finish with 2 rows Plum. For weaving details refer to the previous scarf, Funky Houndstooth.

Finishing:
Work a twisted fringe dividing ends in 5 groups of approximately the same size.

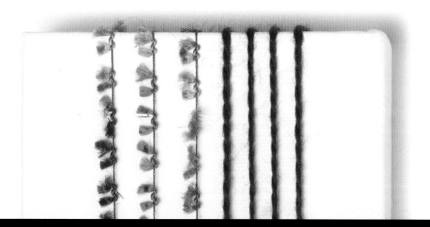

The stripes and squares in this work are formed with different textures in shades of green and blue. Four thick shaggy lines of a blue random colour yarn run down the length of the scarf. Enjoy creating your own original art-scarf!

Yarn Used:
Poof from Crystal Palace – 43 m/47 yds = 50 gms
Squiggle from Crystal Palace – 91.5 m/100 yds = 50 gms
Tekapo from Ashford – 200 m/218 yds = 100 gms

Quantity:
Poof – 1 x 50 gm ball in Blue Jeans, colour #9664
Squiggle – 1 x 50 gm ball in Skuba Dive, colour #9548
Tekapo yarn – approx. 50 gms in Jungle Green,
        colour # 039 and 50 gms in Lime,
        colour # 035

Warp:
Length – 190 cm (75 ins)
Number of ends – 26
Finished width – 11.5 cm (4 ½ ins)

Warp Yarn:
Use Tekapo in Lime and Poof in Blue Jeans

Warp Sequence:
7 Lime
1 Blue
1 Lime
1 Blue
5 Lime
1 Blue
1 Lime
1 Blue
8 Lime

When placing 1 accent thread (in this case the thick blue thread) into the warp it is necessary to cut and join the yarns at the peg and the back of the loom.

The Weaving:
Wind one shuttle with the Jungle Green and one with the Squiggle. Weave random amounts of each yarn to give the scarf a natural sea-scape effect. For example, I started as follows:
6 rows Squiggle,
20 rows Jungle Green
4 rows Squiggle
10 rows Jungle Green
12 rows Squiggle .... continuing in your own way.
When using the Squiggle yarn pull the little tails up to the surface of the weaving before beating the row into place.
Beat gently – Tekapo 5 rows to 2.5 cm (1 in.)
                Squiggle 7 rows to 2.5 cm (1 in.)

Finishing:
Tie ends in groups of 3 or 4. Do it randomly and try not to count. This will add to the artistic "look" of this woven piece.

This scarf is designed to give you a go at playing with colours. You will see how different colours change and intermingle as they cross each other in the warp and weft. Use bright colours so the different effects really show up in the weaving.

Yarn Used:

Any smooth DK sportsweight yarn is fine for this project. Maybe you can take a look in your stash and see what you can find.

Colours used – Red, Teal, Apple Green, Pumpkin, Bright Random, Jungle Green.

Yarns in this project are all from the Tekapo DK range.

Quantity:

A little more than 10 gms (1/2 oz) of each colour.

Tekapo colours – Red # 008, Teal # 037,
Apple Green # 013, Pumpkin #022, Jungle Green # 039 and Random colour Summertimes # 039

Warp:

Length – 190 cm (75 ins)
Number of ends – 52
Finished width – 16 cm (6 1/2 ins)

Warp Sequence:

The warp was threaded in 3 sections.
Each section is a different colour block.
When you have finished each colour sequence, cut and tie the new colours at the back stick.

First section – 18 Random
Second section – 18 Bright Red
Third section – 2 Teal and 2 Apple Green alternate (16 ends)
Tie Teal and Apple Green to the Bright Red and take each colour one at a time through the slots.

1	2	3
Random	Bright Red	2 Teal/ 2 Apple Green

The Weaving:

There are seven areas of pattern as follows. Repeat sequence in each group for 19 cm (7 1/2 ins)

1. 1 Mid Green, 1 Orange
2. 1 Apple Green, 2 Random
3. 3 Random, 1 Orange
4. 3 Teal, 1 Orange
5. 2 Teal, 2 Apple green
6. Red
7. Random – Work to end leaving 23 cm (9 ins) at end for fringe.

Remember – when using 2 different colours don't forget to go around a colour when you meet it at the edge.

Finishing:

A twisted fringe looks very smart and shows up all the colours very well.

White on white works well in weaving. The textures of the different yarns, here, a natural fibre and man-made fibre, look good together in a simple stripe design.

Yarns Used:
Boa from Bernat – 65 m/71 yds = 50 gms
Tekapo from Ashford – 200 m/218 yds = 100 gms

Quantity:
Boa – 1 x 50 gm ball in White
Tekapo – 50 gms in Natural White

Warp:
Length – 190 cm (75 ins)
Number of ends – 38
Finished Width – 11.5 cm (4 1/2 ins)

Warp Yarn:
Boa x 2, and Tekapo x 4.
Repeat across warp, 6 sections of Tekapo and 7 lines of Boa.
There will be Boa yarn at each edge.
(When making a warp with 2 colours, refer to page 12.)

The Weaving:
Use Tekapo throughout.
Beat softly, 13 rows = 5 cm (2 ins).

Finishing:
Tie ends in groups of 4 with 5 at each edge.
Use overhand knots.

Let the Yarns do the Talking

Sometimes it's worthwhile keeping things simple and letting the yarns make the design. The random-dyed yarns are especially useful in this context. A variety of random dyed yarns have been used in these projects – ribbon, eyelash, a pigtail yarn, a textured handspun look yarn and a smooth wool yarn. They all show off their qualities in a very different way.

Let the Yarns do the Talking | *1* *Fun and Squiggle*

The plain textured colours in the background really show off the pigtail Squiggle yarn.

Yarn Used:
Squiggle from Crystal Palace – 139 m/152 yds = 50 gms
Fizz from Crystal Palace – 110 m/120 yds = 50 gms
Tekapo from Ashford – 200 m/218 yds = 100 gms

Quantity:
Version one
Squiggle – 1 x 50 gm ball in Fern Mix, colour # 9210
Fizz – 1 x 50 gm ball in Key Lime, colour # 9224
Tekapo – approx. 35 gms in Plum, colour # 010

Version two
Squiggle – 1 x 50 gm ball in Circus, colour # 9297
Fizz – 1 x 50 gm ball in Orangeade, colour # 9220
Tekapo – approx. 35 gms in Violet, colour # 036

Warp:
Length – 190 cm (75 ins)
Number of ends – 40
Finished width – 11.5 cm (4 ¹/₂ ins)

Warp Yarn:
Tekapo x 4 and Fizz x 2, repeat across warp, finish with Tekapo x 4.
7 sections of Tekapo and 6 lines of Fizz. There will be Tekapo yarn at each edge.
Tie both colours to the back stick and leave them there until that colour is needed to go through the slot. No need to cut and tie at each colour change.

The Weaving:
Use Squiggle throughout.
Pull the little tails of Squiggle yarn up to the surface of the weaving before beating the row into place.
Beat gently! It is very easy to beat the Squiggle yarn down too much.
7 rows to 2.5 cm (1 in.).

Finishing:
Tie ends in groups of 6, 4 Tekapo and 2 Fizz, except one edge where you will have only 4 x Tekapo.

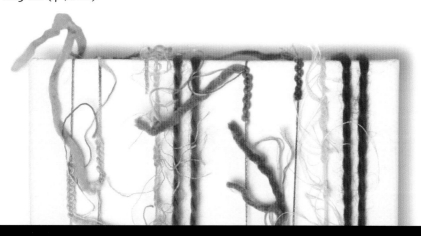

Use a smooth yarn, a random-dyed in both the warp and the weft. The design will form automatically. It will be your own original pattern. Make a second scarf in the same way but change the number of warp ends and you will be surprised to see a new pattern emerge.

Yarn Used:
Use any smooth DK Sportsweight yarn in a pretty, random-dyed shade.
I used Ashford Tekapo in random colour Wisteria – 200 m/218 yds = 100 gms

Quantity:
DK Sportsweight yarn approx. 90 gm

Warp:
Length – 190 cm (75 ins)
Number of ends – 40
Finished width – 12.5 cm (5 ins)

Warp Yarn:
Sportsweight DK throughout.
Beat into a square balanced weave – the same number of rows up as across.

The Weaving:
Same yarn as warp. Wind as much as you can onto the shuttle so you don't break the pattern sequence that forms, by joining the yarn during the weaving.
Beat so you have the same number of rows up as you do across. This is called a balanced weave.

Finishing:
Make a twisted fringe, 4 ends in each group.

Let the Yarns do the Talking | 3 Lollipop

A random-dyed textured yarn was used in a hot pink/snowy white mix. The dyed colours form their own pattern and the boucle texture of the yarn adds another dimension to the overall result.

Yarn Used:
Lollipop boucle by Magic Garden – 110 m/120 yds = 50 gms

Quantity:
Lollipop – 2 x 50 gm balls in Pink and White, colour # 703.

Warp:
Length – 190 cm (75 ins)
Number of ends – 48
Finished width – 12 cm (4 3/4 ins)

Warp Yarn:
Lollipop used throughout.

The Weaving:
Use same yarn as warp. Beat so you have the same number of rows up as you do across. This is called a balanced weave.

Finishing:
Tie ends in groups of 6 using overhand knots.

Three dramatic colours and unique yarns combine to make a very exotic-looking scarf. The black stripes in the ribbon yarn really add to the overall effect. The Optik yarn used in the weft is a wonderful mix of cotton, acrylic, mohair, metallic and polyester in different textures along the length of the yarn.

Yarn Used:
Optik from Berroco – 80 m/87 yds = 50 gms
Deco-Ribbon from Crystal Palace – 73 m/80 yds = 50 gms
Rare Earth 12 ply boucle Alpaca from Rare Yarns – 100 m/110 yds – 50 gms

Quantity:
Optik – 1 x 50 gm hank in colour # 4945
Deco-Ribbon – 1 x 50 gm ball in Black, colour # 106
Rare Earth Alpaca – 1 x 50 gm ball in Black

Warp:
Length – 190 cm (75 ins)
Number of ends – 38
Finished width – 12.5 cm (5 ins)

Warp Yarn:
Alpaca x 2 and Deco Ribbon x 2 repeat across warp. Finish with 2 alpaca. There will be alpaca at each edge.
(When making a warp with 2 colours, refer to page 12.)

The Weaving:
Use Optik throughout. Enjoy seeing all the textures appearing as you weave. Beat at 5 rows to 2.5 cm (1 in.).

Finishing:
Tie end in groups of 4 with a group of 5 at each edge. Use overhand knots.

The eyelash yarns are fun to use and they are knotted into the weave to make a flouncy little edge on the ends of the scarf. The random colours of the eyelash are carried through the whole work and the rusty background colour brings out the beautiful peacock colours.

Yarn Used:
Temptation from Wentworth – 60 m/66 yds = 50 gms
Tekapo from Ashford – 200 m/218 yds = 100 gms

Quantity:
Temptation – 1 x 50 gm ball in Random, colour # 501
Tekapo – 1 x 100 gm ball in Copper, colour # 030
Every piece of the Temptation was used. You may need to break into another ball.

Warp:
Length – 185 cm (73 ins)
Number of ends – 42
Finished width – 14 cm (5 ½ ins)

Warp Yarn:
Use Tekapo throughout.

The Weaving:
The eyelash yarn is placed into the weave in a series of knots. There are 3 rows of knots at each end of the scarf.
You will need 42 lengths of Temptation eyelash yarn – 19 cm (7 ½ ins) long for each row of knots.
A quick way to do this is to cut a piece of thin card 9.5 cm (3 ¾ ins) wide and wrap the eyelash yarn around the length of the card 21 times. Use sharp scissors to cut the yarn along the edge of the card. This makes 21 lengths 19 cm (7 ½ ins) long.
Do this 6 times to make enough for 6 rows of knots.
Wind the rest of the Temptation and the Tekapo yarn onto the shuttle together.

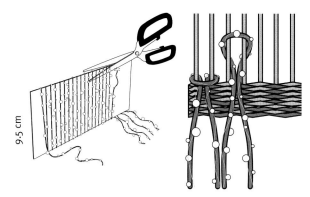

9.5 cm

Start the Weaving:
Weave 2 rows.
Don't cut the yarn, just leave the shuttle at the side of the loom while the knots are laid in place.

Placing the Knots:
Put the reed into the rest position when placing the knots. Take 2 ready-cut lengths of eyelash yarn.
Place them around 2 warp threads to make a knot – see sketch.
Continue to place the knots in this way across the row. Weave 6 rows.
Work another row of knots as before.
Repeat the above 2 lines twice (3 rows of knots)
Weave to within 36 cm (14 ins) of the end of the warp. Put the reed into the rest position.
Place a row of knots, as you did before, across the row. Weave 6 rows. Repeat as before (2 rows of knots + 6 rows of weaving)
Place the final row of knots. Weave 2 rows. You are finished the weaving! Remove weaving from loom.

Finishing:
Tie Tekapo ends in groups of 2. Use overhand knots. Trim these ends just a little shorter than the eyelash fringe.

Exotic & Luxurious

There are a great number of exotic yarns to enjoy. Silk, alpaca, cashmere, cotton and fine merinos have a special feel and nature of their own. Each project will give you a different taste of how these yarns can be used.

Exotic & Luxurious | 1 | *Merino Tweed*

This scarf has the warm, soft feel of merino and the pattern looks very high-tech but is really very simple.

Yarn Used:
Extra from Stampato – 90 m/98 yds = 50 gms
Feeling from Lana Gatto – 140 m/153 yds = 50 gms

Quantity:
Extra – 1 x 50 gm ball in Random, colour # 8008
Feeling – 1 x 50 gm ball in Rust, colour # 12946
I also tried the Red, colour # 10095, and it looked very good too.

Warp:
Length – 160 cm (63 ins)
Number of ends – 50
Finished width – 14.5 cm (5 3/4 ins)

Warp Yarn:
Rust x 2 and Random colour x 2, repeat across row, ending with Rust x 2. There will be Rust colour at both edges.
(When making a warp with 2 colours, refer to page 12.)

The Weaving:
Weave Rust x 1 and Random x 1 throughout length. Always remember to go around the other colour when you meet it at the edge. You will find it tricky for a start but you will find it comes naturally after you have done a few rows. *(Refer to weaving notes page 12.)*
Beat into a perfectly square weave. The rows up will equal the number of rows across. This is a balanced weave.

Finishing:
Make a twisted fringe in groups of 4. The two edge groups will have 5 threads.

The cotton yarns give a very different, clear and simple look. There is no elasticity in the yarn so take care with your edges and beat a little more than usual.

Yarn Used:
Butterfly Mercerized Cotton from Mouzakis – 230 m/ 250 yds = 125 gms
Kelly Cotton/Acrylic from King – 98 m/107 yds = 50 gms

Quantity:
Butterfly – 1 x 125 gm ball in Grey, colour # 3033
Kelly – 1 x 50 gm ball in random, colour # 62

Warp:
Length – 165 cm (65 ins)
Number of ends – 40
Finished width – 12 cm (4 3/4 ins)

Warp Yarn:
Use Kelly random colour throughout.

The Weaving:
Use Butterfly throughout.
Beat 5 to 6 rows to 2.5 cm (1 in.).

Finishing:
Make a twisted fringe in groups of 4 threads.

The Alpaca scarf is so soft and cosy to have around your neck. I have used natural colours that sit very well together.

Yarn Used:

Alpaca from Classic – 100 m/110 yds = 50 gms
Rare Earth from Rare Yarns Alpaca – 110 m/120 yds = 50 gms

Quantity:

Classic Alpaca –
   1 x 50 gm ball in Silver Grey, colour # 401
   1 x 50 gm ball in Warm Brown, colour # 207
   1 x 50 gm ball in Brown, colour # 211
Rare Earth Alpaca/Boucle – 1 x 50 gm ball in Pacific Weave, colour # 004

Warp:

Length – 180 cm (71 ins)
Number of ends – 48
Finished width – 14 cm (5 ½ ins)

Warp Yarn:

Use the 2 Classic Alpaca yarns, Warm Brown and Brown. The warp is threaded in 3 sections. Each section is a different colour block.
First section: 2 Warm Brown and 2 Brown alternate (16 ends)
Second section: 16 Warm Brown
Third section: 2 Brown and 2 Warm Brown (16 ends)

2 Warm Brown and 2 Brown	All Warm Brown	2 Brown and 2 Warm Brown

(When making a warp with 2 colours, refer to page 12.)

The Weaving:

Combine 2 yarns, Silver Grey and boucle, together on the shuttle. Weave throughout with these 2 yarns together.
Beat gently 9 rows to 5 cm (2 ins).

Finishing:

Make a twisted fringe in groups of 4 threads.

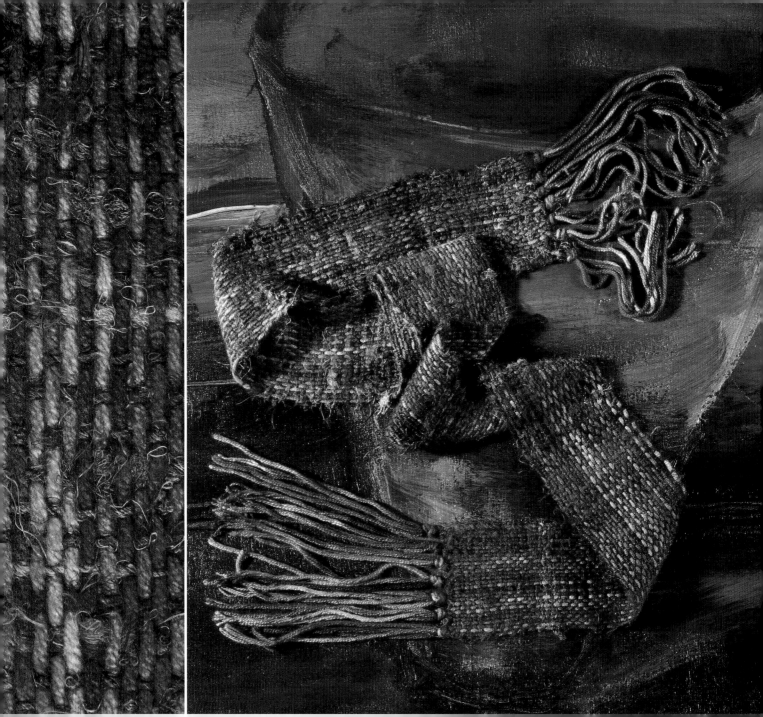

This project is very decorative. Wear this narrow scarf with a coat or under a collar as a striking accent. Use a super-soft warp yarn to give the silk the flexibility needed to drape nicely around your neck.

Yarn Used:
Hand-dyed Silk/Cashmere from Fleece Artist – 80 m/ 87 yds = 50 gms
Recycled Silk from Mango Moon – 137 m/150 yds = 175 gms

Quantity:
Hand-dyed yarn – 1 x 50 gm ball
Recycled silk – approx. 40 gms

Warp:
Length – 200 cm (78 3/4 ins)
Number of ends – 28
Finished width – 8 cm (just over 3 ins)

Warp Yarn:
Use hand-dyed silk/cashmere.

The Weaving:
Use recycled silk throughout. Beat softly.

Finishing:
Tie ends in groups of 4.
Use an overhand knot.

Faux Ikat

You can find self-patterning sock yarn in every colour imaginable. The pattern is predetermined in the dye pot, so when you knit or weave, the pattern forms automatically. When this yarn is woven it forms an ikat/ tie-dyed look. Ikat is an ancient technique used in hand weaving in a few countries around the world. The technique was developed to create pattern and design when dyeing the yarn, rather than in the weaving. These projects have used the sock yarn, adding some texture for accent to make some interesting faux ikat patterns.

Faux Ikat | *1* *Pretty Pink*

The Alpaca/Merino warp gives the scarf a very soft, warm feel.

Yarn Used:
Opal Sock yarn – 425 m/464 yds = 100 gms
Alpaca/Merino yarn Standard DK Sportsweight – 100 m /110 yds = 50 gms

Quantity:
Opal – 1/2 x 100 gm ball in Elemente design, colour # 1071
Alpaca/Merino – 1 x 50 gm ball. A friend gave me this yarn without a label. Choose any soft DK alpaca yarn.

Warp:
Length – 190 cm (75 ins)
Number of ends – 42
Finished width – 12 cm (4 3/4 ins)

Warp Yarn:
Alpaca/Merino throughout.

The Weaving:
Use Opal throughout.
Beat 15 rows to 5 cm (2 ins).

Finishing:
Make a twisted fringe 4 ends in each group – 5 ends at each edge.

Faux Ikat | 2   *Shades of Gold*

This scarf has a little texture added into the warp in the grey/white colours of the yarn pattern. The solid colour in the yarn was gold so I chose a plain gold yarn for the warp.

Yarn Used:
Opal Sock yarn – 425 m/464 yds = 100 gms
Fizz from Crystal Palace – 110 m/120 yds = 50 gms
DK Sportsweight yarn – 200 m/218 yds = 100 gms
The scarf will be softer if you choose a DK yarn with some alpaca or cashmere content.

Quantity:
Opal – 1/2 x 100 gm ball in Brazil design, colour # 1073
Fizz – 6 lengths x 190 cm (75 ins) per length in Newsprint, colour # 9413
DK yarn x 50 gms in gold to match the gold in the Opal yarn.

Warp:
Length – 190 cm (75 ins)
Number of ends – 40
Finished width – 11.5 cm (4 ¹/₂ ins)

Warp Yarn:
Gold yarn used across the warp. When you have all the gold threads laid in, add 3 Fizz threads at random across the warp. Place them in the same slot as a gold yarn. Separate one of these into a hole in the reed along with the gold yarn when you do the threading process.

The Weaving:
Use Opal throughout.
Beat 15 rows to 5 cm (2 ins)

Finishing:
Tie ends in groups of 4 with a group of 5 at each edge. Use overhand knots.

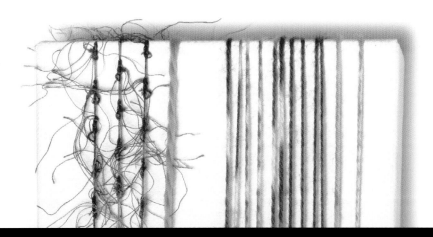

The green printed yarn with the black as a warp shows off the pattern in the yarn.

Yarn Used:
Opal Sock yarn – 425 m/464 yds = 100 gms
DK Sportsweight yarn – 200 m/218 yds = 100 gms
The scarf will be softer if you choose a DK yarn with some alpaca or cashmere content.

Quantity:
Opal – approx. 70 gms in Brazil design, colour # 5004
DK Sportsweight yarn – 50 gms in black

Warp:
Length – 190 cm (75 ins)
Number of ends – 42
Finished width – 11 cm (4 1/4 ins)

Warp Yarn:
Use black DK throughout.

The Weaving:
Use Opal throughout.
Beat – 15 rows to 5 cm (2 ins).

Finishing:
Make a twisted fringe, 4 ends in each group and 5 ends at each edge.

This self-patterning sock yarn is such fun to use I had to try one more idea, hence an extra scarf in this group. I chose an Opal yarn with a bright lavender blue accent and added an icy white textured yarn.

Yarn Used:
Opal Sock yarn – 425 m/464 yds = 100 gms
Créme de la Créme from Patons – 91 m/99 yds = 50 gms

Quantity:
Opal – 1 x 100 gm ball in Elemente Design, colour # 1075
Créme de la Créme – ½ ball in Icy White, colour # 1000

Warp:
Length – 190 cm (75 ins)
Number of ends – 46
Finished width – 13 cm (5 ins)

Warp Yarns:
Use Opal and Icy White yarn.

Warp Sequence:
Opal x 6
White x 2
Repeat 5 times and finish with 6 Opal. There will be 6 Opal at each edge.

The Weaving:
The idea was to use the white fancy yarn to mark the areas of colour. Each time, as the colour of the Opal changes weave one row of the white. Leave the white thread at the edge and carry it up the selvedge as you weave the Opal, i.e., every time you meet the white, go around it and into the next row. It will always be at the side ready for when you need it. *(Refer to weaving notes on page 12.)*

Beat 15 rows to 5cm (2 ins).

Finishing:
Tie ends in random numbers of ends.
Use overhand knots.

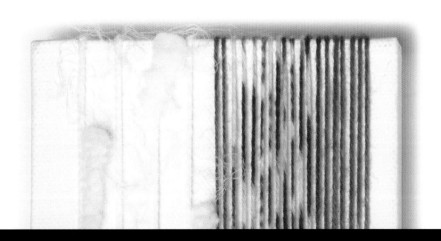

The bright sock yarn with a distinct pattern lent itself to a wider piece of weaving. The colours are accented by the addition of 4 bright colours into the warp.

Yarn Used:
Opal sock yarn – 425 m/464 yds = 100 gms
Tekapo from Ashford – 200 m/218 yds = 100 gms

Quantity:
Opal – 1 x 100 gm ball in Rodeo design, colour # 1153
Tekapo yarn –

Bright Yellow, colour # 017 x 2 lengths of 190 cm/75 ins each

Bright Violet, colour # 036 x 4 lengths of 190 cm/75 ins each

Bright Orange, colour # 022 x 4 lengths of 190 cm/75 ins each

Bright Green, colour # 013 x 2 lengths of 190 cm/75 ins each

Choose colours as bright as possible to enhance the colours in the sock yarn.

Warp:
Length – 190 cm (75 ins)
Number of ends – 50 x double and 12 single = 112 total
Finished width – 17 cm (6 3/4 ins)

Warp Yarn:
Opal and DK yarn.

Warp Sequence:
Place the Opal yarn in each slot and hole. This doubles up the yarn across the warp.
Place the DK yarn in as usual – only in a slot – see sketch in previous scarf , Brazil.

Stripes Laid As Follows

Purple 2	10 Double	Orange 2	10 Double	Yellow 2	10 Double	Green 2	10 Double	Orange 2	10 Double	Purple 2

I laid the Opal yarn in first, then took each bright colour through a slot over the peg and tied it to itself at the back stick. Repeat this for each bright colour.

Threading:
You will only need to move the bright DK threads into a hole. Opal yarn is already in a hole and a slot.

The Weaving:
Use Opal throughout. Beat 15 rows to 5 cm (2 ins).

Finishing:
Tie ends using overhand knots – approx. 8 ends in each group.

Faux Ikat | 6 *Brazil*

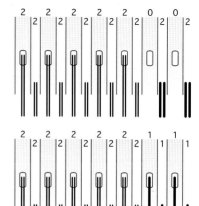

The warp threads are laid closer together which alters the design. The 2 white stripes really help the bright colours to stand out and form the very distinctive pattern.

Yarn Used:
Opal Sock yarn – 425 m/464 yds = 100 gms
DK Sportsweight yarn – 200 m/218 yds = 100 gms

Quantity:
Opal – 1 x 100 gm ball in Brazil design, colour # 5001
DK Sportsweight yarn – 8 lengths x 190 cm (75 ins) per length in white

Warp:
Length – 190 cm (75 ins)
Number of ends – 30 x double and 8 single = 68 in total
Finished width – 11 cm (4 ¼ ins)

Warp Yarn:
Use Opal yarn and white DK yarn.

Warp Sequence:
Place the Opal yarn in each slot and hole. This doubles up the yarn across the warp.
Place the DK white in as usual, only in a slot.

Sequence:
Opal – 10 double
White – 4
Opal – 10 double
White – 4
Opal – 10 double

Threading:
You will only need to move the 2 stripes of 4 white threads into a hole. The Opal yarn is already in a hole and a slot.

The Weaving:
Use Opal throughout.
Beat – 15 rows to 5 cm (2 ins).

Finishing:
Make a twisted fringe in 17 groups.

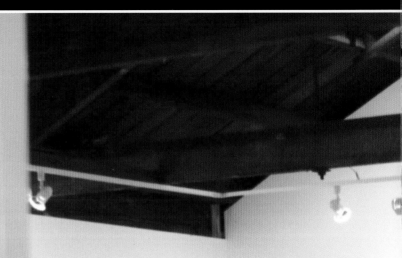

Yarns used in the projects

Yarn name	Company name	Type of yarn	Content
Boa	Bernat	Shiny Eyelash Yarn	100% Polyester
Boucle	Lion	Bulky Boucle	79% Polyester/20% Mohair/1% Polyester
Butterfly	Mouzakis	Mercerised Cotton	100% Mercerised Cotton
Circus	Wentworth	Fancy Knot and Eyelash Yarn	55% Polymide/45% Polyester
Classic Alpaca	America Alpaca	DK Yarn	100% Alpaca
Créme de la Créme	Patons	Bumpy super soft yarn	52% Tactel/48% Nylon
Deco Ribbon	Crystal Palace	Striped Ribbon Yarn	70% Acrylic/30% Nylon
Extra	Feeling	DK Sportsweight	100% Merino Wool
Feeling	Lana Gatto	DK Sportsweight	70% Merino/20% Silk/10% Cashmere
Fizz	Crystal Palace	Eyelash yarn	100% Polyester
Hand dyed Silk	Fleece Artist	KK Yarn	50% Cashmere/50% silk
Kelly	King	Fine DK Yarn	55% Cotton/45%Acrylic
La Gran	Classic Elite	Brushed Mohair	76.5% Mohair/6% Nylon/17.5% Wool
Little Flowers	Crystal Palace	Fancy Yarn	66% Rayon/30% Nylon/4% Metallic Fibres
Lollipop	Magic Garden	Fine Boucle	95% Merino wool/5% Wool/Nylon blend
Loopy	Patons	Big Loop Yarn	83% Mohair/17% Acrylic
Optik	Berroco	Fancy Yarn	48% Cotton/21% Acrylic/20% Mohair/8% Metallic/3% Polyester
Ostrich	Patons	Long Eyelash	100% Polyester
Parade	Classic Elite	Bulky Knotty	82% Nylon/18% Acrylic
Poof	Crystal Palace	Chunky Fleecy Yarn	100% Microfibre
Rare Earth Alpaca	Rare Yarns	DK Sportsweight	100% Alpaca
Recycled Silk	Mango Moon	Fancy Yarn	100% Silk
Sock Yarn	Opal	Fibe 4 ply	75% Wool/25% Polymide
Squiggle	Crystal Palace	Pigtail Yarn	50% Nylon/50% Polyester
Tekapo	Ashford	DK Sportsweight	100% Wool
Temptation	Wentworth	Long Eyelash	100% Polyester

If you can't find the exact yarn, try something close. You may discover something new and exciting. That is the magic of weaving!!